SOUTHERN COOKING

GALLERY BOOKS
An Imprint of W. H. Smith Publishers Inc.
112 Madison Avenue
New York City 10016

D1361350

INTRODUCTION

A thread of similarity runs through the cuisine of America in all its regional forms, modified slightly by the regions themselves, by the people who settled there, the crops they found or cultivated and the indigenous game of the forest or fish of rivers and sea. The South, of course, has its specialties, all with their own particular style and yet all particularly American.

Famous in history for its gracious living, elegant plantation houses and lavish entertaining, the South is also known for its farming heritage, with its hearty, unpretentious fare made up of whatever the cook had to hand, simmered slowly while the work of the day went on. These stews are every bit as satisfying as those of provincial France, and deserve to be better known. The area of the United States that calls itself the South takes in a lot of territory down the Eastern Seaboard and around the Gulf of Mexico, along the Mississippi, through the mountains of Arkansas and Tennessee and into the rolling hills of Kentucky. But wherever you go in this region, there are familiar foods like biscuits or corn muffins that can't be surpassed anywhere, and that make you feel instantly at home.

SERVES 4-6

CORN AND POTATO CHOWDER

Such a filling soup, this is really a
complete meal in a bowl. Corn is a
favorite ingredient in Southern cooking.

6 medium potatoes, peeled
Chicken or vegetable stock
1 onion, finely chopped
2 tbsps butter or margarine
1 tbsp flour
4oz cooked ham, chopped
4 ears fresh corn or about 4oz canned or frozen corn
3 cups milk
Salt and dash tabasco
Finely chopped parsley

1. Quarter the potatoes and place them in a deep sauce-pan. Add stock to cover and the onion, and bring the mixture to the boil. Lower the heat and simmer, partially covered, until the potatoes are soft, about 15-20 minutes.

2. Drain the potatoes, reserving ¾ pint of the cooking liquid. Mash the potatoes and combine with reserved liquid.

3. Melt the butter or margarine in a clean pan, add the ham and cook briefly. Stir in the flour and pour over the potato mixture, mixing well.

4. If using fresh corn, remove the husks and silk and, holding one end of the corn, stand the ear upright. Use a large, sharp knife and cut against the cob vertically from top to bottom just scraping off the kernels. Add the corn and milk to the potato mixture and bring almost to the boil. Do not boil the corn rapidly as this will toughen it. Add a pinch of salt and a dash of tabasco, and garnish with parsley before serving.

Step 3 Pour the potato mixture onto the flour and ham gradually, stirring constantly until well blended.

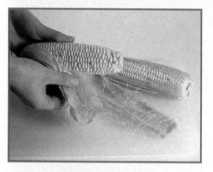

Step 4 Remove the husks and silk from the ears of corn.

Step 4 Use a sharp knife to cut the kernels off the cobs.

Cook's Notes

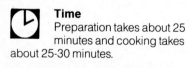 **Time**
Preparation takes about 25 minutes and cooking takes about 25-30 minutes.

 **Preparation**
The soup may be prepared in advance up to adding the corn. Bring the mixture to a rapid boil. turn down the heat and then add the corn and continue with the recipe. This soup does not freeze well.

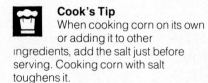 **Cook's Tip**
When cooking corn on its own or adding it to other ingredients, add the salt just before serving. Cooking corn with salt toughens it.

SERVES 4

VIRGINIA PEANUT SOUP

Peanuts, popular all over the South,
make a velvety rich soup that is easily
made from ordinary store cupboard ingredients.

4 tbsps butter or margarine
2 tbsps flour
1 cup creamy peanut butter
¼ tsp celery seed
2½ cups chicken stock
½ cup dry sherry
½ cup coarsely chopped peanuts

Step 4 Add the sherry to the soup before serving.

Step 2 Once the peanut butter and celery seed are added, gradually pour in the stock, stirring or whisking constantly.

1. Melt the butter or margarine in a medium saucepan. Remove from the heat and stir in the flour.

2. Add the peanut butter and celery seed. Gradually pour on the stock, stirring constantly.

3. Return the pan to the heat and simmer gently for about 15 minutes. Do not allow to boil rapidly.

4. Stir in the sherry and ladle into a tureen or individual bowls. Sprinkle with the chopped peanuts.

Cook's Notes

 Time
Preparation takes about 15 minutes and cooking takes about 15 minutes.

 Variation
For a crunchier texture, add 2 sticks of finely diced celery to the butter or margarine and cook until slightly softened before adding the flour.

 Preparation
The soup is slightly difficult to reheat, so it is best prepared just before serving.

SERVES 4

SHE CRAB SOUP

A female crab, with roe intact, is needed
for a truly authentic soup. However, exceptions
can be made with results just as delicious.

1 large crab, cooked
3 tbsps butter or margarine
1 onion, very finely chopped
2 tbsps flour
4 cups milk
6 tbsps sherry
Pinch salt, white pepper and ground mace
½ cup heavy cream, whipped
Red caviar

1. To dress the crab, take off all the legs and the large claws. Crack the large claws and legs and extract the meat.

2. Turn the crab shell over and press up with thumbs to push out the underbody. Cut this piece in quarters and use a skewer to pick out the meat. Discard the stomach sac and the lungs (dead man's fingers). Set the white meat aside with the claw meat.

3. Using a teaspoon, scrape out the brown meat from inside the shell and reserve it. If the roe is present reserve that, too.

4. Melt the butter or margarine in a medium saucepan and soften the onion for about 3 minutes. Do not allow to brown.

5. Stir in the flour and milk. Bring to the boil and then immediately turn down the heat to simmer. Add the brown meat from the crab and cook gently for about 20 minutes.

6. Add the sherry, salt, pepper, mace, white crab meat and roe. Cook a further 5 minutes.

7. Top each serving with a spoonful of whipped cream and red caviar.

Step 1 Remove the legs and large claws of the crab. Use a rolling pin or meat mallet to crack the large claws and legs to extract the meat.

Step 2 Turn the crab shell over and push out the underbody. Discard stomach sac and lungs.

Step 3 Using a teaspoon, scrape out the brown meat from inside the shell.

Cook's Notes

Time
Preparation takes about 35-40 minutes and cooking takes about 25 minutes.

Variation
Frozen crab meat may be substituted. Use about 4-6oz of white crab meat and omit the addition of the brown body meat. Do not use a dressed crab as the brown meat will usually have breadcrumbs added to it.

Buying Guide
Crabs are available freshly boiled from fishmongers. Buy a crab that is heavy for its size.

SERVES 2-4

SEA ISLAND SHRIMP

Although this is a recipe from the
Carolinas, it is popular everywhere
succulent shrimp are available.

2 dozen raw large shrimp, unpeeled
4 tbsps butter or margarine
1 small red pepper, seeded and finely chopped
2 green onions, finely chopped
½ tsp dry mustard
2 tsps dry sherry
1 tsp Worcester sauce
4oz cooked crab meat
6 tbsps fresh breadcrumbs
1 tbsp chopped parsley
2 tbsps mayonnaise
Salt and pepper
1 small egg, beaten
Grated Parmesan cheese
Paprika

1. Remove all of the shrimp shells except for the very tail ends.

2. Remove the black veins on the rounded sides.

3. Cut the shrimp down the length of the curved side and press each one open.

4. Melt half of the butter or margarine in a small pan and cook the pepper to soften, about 3 minutes. Add the green onions and cook a further 2 minutes.

5. Combine the peppers with the mustard, sherry, Worcester sauce, crab meat, breadcrumbs, parsley and mayonnaise. Add seasoning and enough egg to bind together.

6. Spoon the stuffing onto the shrimp and sprinkle with the Parmesan cheese and paprika. Melt the remaining butter or margarine and drizzle over the shrimp.

7. Bake in a pre-heated 350°F oven for about 10 minutes. Serve immediately.

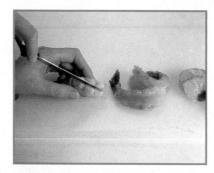

Step 3 Cut the shrimp down the length of the curved side and press each one open.

Step 6 Spoon the stuffing into the shrimp, pressing down lightly to spread shrimp open.

Cook's Notes

Time
Preparation takes about 30 minutes and cooking takes about 15 minutes.

Variation
Try chopped black or green olives in the stuffing for a change of flavor. Mushrooms may be cooked with the red pepper and green onions, if desired, and other herbs substituted for parsley.

Serving Ideas
Serve as an appetizer or as a main course for 2 people.

SERVES 2-4

JEKYLL ISLAND SHRIMP

Named for an island off the Georgia
coast, this makes a rich appetizer
or an elegant main course.

2lbs cooked shrimp
4 tbsps butter, softened
Pinch salt, white pepper and cayenne
1 clove garlic, crushed
6 tbsps fine dry breadcrumbs
2 tbsps chopped parsley
4 tbsps sherry
Lemon wedges or slices

Step 2 Pull off the tail shell and carefully remove the very end.

Step 1 Remove the heads and legs from the shrimp first. Remove any roe at this time.

Step 6 Spread the mixture to completely cover the shrimp.

1. To prepare the shrimp, remove the heads and legs first.

2. Peel off the shells, carefully removing the tail shells.

3. Remove the black vein running down the length of the rounded side with a wooden pick.

4. Arrange shrimp in a shallow casserole or individual dishes.

5. Combine the remaining ingredients, except the lemon garnish, mixing well.

6. Spread the mixture to completely cover the shrimp and place in a pre-heated 375°F oven for about 20 minutes, or until the butter melts and the crumbs become crisp. Garnish with lemon wedges or slices.

Cook's Notes

 Time
Preparation takes about 35-40 minutes and cooking takes about 20 minutes.

 Buying Guide
Freshly cooked shrimp are available from most fishmongers. Frozen shrimp will not be as good.

SERVES 4

OREGANO OYSTERS

The combination of oregano and the anise taste
of Pernod is an unusual but very complementary
one, especially with fresh oysters.

Step 2 Using a small, sharp knife, loosen the oyster from its shell.

1 tbsp butter or margarine
1 clove garlic, crushed
1 tbsp chopped parsley
1 tbsp chopped fresh oregano or 1½ tsps dried oregano
1 tbsp Pernod
¾ cup heavy cream
Salt and pepper
24 oysters on the half shell
12 strips bacon, cooked and crumbled
Coarse salt

Step 3 Cook mixture until reduced by a quarter.

1. Melt the butter or margarine in a saucepan. Add the garlic and cook to soften, but do not brown.

2. Add the parsley, oregano, Pernod and cream. Bring to the boil and lower the heat to simmering. Strain on any liquid from the oysters and then loosen them from their shells with a small, sharp knife.

3. Cook the mixture until reduced by about one quarter and slightly thickened. Test the seasoning and set the mixture aside.

4. Pour about 1 inch coarse salt into a baking pan.

Step 5 Place the oysters in their shells into the coarse salt, twisting so that they stand level.

5. Place the oysters on top of the salt and twist the shells into the salt so that they stand level.

6. Spoon some of the cream over each oyster and sprinkle with the crumbled bacon.

7. Bake in a pre-heated 400°F oven for 15-18 minutes. Serve immediately.

Cook's Notes

Time
Preparation takes about 25 minutes. Cooking takes about 20-25 minutes including time to cook the bacon.

$ Buying Guide
It is possible to purchase oysters already on the half shell. If you need to open them yourself, buy a special oyster knife with a short, strong blade. Insert the blade at the hinge and twist until shells separate.

Variation
If oysters are unavailable, use mussels or clams.

SERVES 4

SNAPPER WITH FENNEL AND ORANGE SALAD

Red snapper brings Florida to mind. Combined with
oranges, it makes a lovely summer meal.

Oil
4 even-sized red snapper, cleaned, heads and tails on
2 heads fennel
2 oranges
Juice of 1 lemon
3 tbsps light salad oil
Pinch sugar, salt and black pepper

a bowl to catch the juice.

5. Add lemon juice to any orange juice collected in the bowl. Add the oil, salt, pepper and a pinch of sugar, if necessary. Mix well and add the fennel, green herb tops and orange segments, stirring carefully. Broil the fish 3-5 minutes per side, depending on thickness. Serve the fish with the heads and tails on, accompanied by the salad.

Step 1 Make three cuts in the side of each fish for even cooking.

Step 2 Slice the fennel in half and remove the cores.

Step 4 Peel and segment the oranges over a bowl to catch the juice.

1. Brush both sides of the fish with oil and cut three slits in the sides of each. Sprinkle with a little of the lemon juice, reserving the rest.

2. Slice the fennel in half and remove the cores. Slice thinly. Also slice the green tops and chop the feathery herb to use in the dressing.

3. Peel the oranges, removing all the white pith.

4. Cut the oranges into segments. Peel and segment over

Cook's Notes

Time
Preparation takes about 30 minutes and cooking takes about 6-10 minutes.

Variation
Other fish may be used in the recipe if snapper is not available. Substitute red mullet or any of the exotic fish from the Seychelles Islands or Hawaii.

Cook's Tip
When broiling whole fish, making several cuts on the side of each fish will help to cook it quickly and evenly throughout.

SERVES 4

Broiled Flounder

A mayonnaise-like topping puffs
to a golden brown to give this mild-
flavored fish a piquant taste.

4 double fillets of flounder
2 eggs, separated
Pinch salt, pepper and dry mustard
1 cup peanut oil
4 tbsps pickle relish
1 tbsp chopped parsley
1 tbsp lemon juice
Dash tabasco

1. Place the egg yolks in a blender, food processor or deep bowl.

2. Blend in the salt, pepper and mustard. If blending by hand, use a small whisk.

3. If using the machine, pour the oil through the funnel in a thin, steady stream with the machine running. If mixing by hand, add oil a few drops at a time, beating well in between each addition.

4. When half the oil has been added, the rest may be added in a thin steady stream while beating constantly with a small whisk.

5. Mix in the relish, parsley, lemon juice and tabasco. Beat the egg whites until stiff but not dry and fold into the mayonnaise.

6. Broil the fish about 2 inches from the heat source for about 6-10 minutes, depending on the thickness of the fillets.

7. Spread the sauce over each fillet and broil for 3-5 minutes longer, or until the sauce puffs and browns lightly.

Step 4 Add the oil to the egg yolk mixture in a thin, steady stream while beating constantly.

Step 5 Fold stiffly-beaten egg whites thoroughly into the mayonnaise.

Step 7 Spread or spoon the sauce over each fish fillet before broiling.

Cook's Notes

Time
Preparation takes about 20 minutes. If preparing the mayonnaise by hand this will take about 15-20 minutes. The fish takes 9-15 minutes to cook.

Watchpoint
When preparing the mayonnaise either by machine or by hand, do not add the oil too quickly or the mayonnaise will curdle. If it does curdle, beat another egg yolk in a bowl and gradually beat in the curdled mixture. This should bring it back together again.

Variation
This same topping may be used on other fish besides flounder.

Serving Ideas
Serve with broiled tomatoes.

SERVES 4

River Inn Quail

Definitely a dish for special occasions,
this is deceptively simple, impressive
and perfect for entertaining.

12 dressed quail
6 tbsps butter
3 tbsps oil
1 clove garlic, crushed
4oz mushrooms, sliced
4 tbsps chopped pecans or walnuts
4 tbsps raisins
1 cup chicken stock
Salt and pepper
3 tbsps sherry
1 tbsp cornstarch
1 tsp tomato paste (optional)
1 bunch watercress

1. Rub each quail inside and out with butter.

2. Pour the oil into a baking pan large enough to hold the quail comfortably. Cook in a pre-heated 350°F oven for about 25 minutes, uncovered.

3. Remove the pan from the oven and place under a pre-heated broiler to brown the quail.

4. Add garlic, mushrooms, pecans, raisins and stock to the quail.

5. Replace in the oven and continue to cook, uncovered, until the quail are tender – a further 20 minutes.

6. Remove the quail and other ingredients to a serving dish, leaving the pan juices behind.

7. Mix the cornstarch and sherry and add it to the pan, stirring constantly.

8. Place the pan over medium heat and cook until the cornstarch thickens and clears. If the baking pan isn't flameproof, transfer the ingredients to a saucepan before thickening the sauce. Add tomato paste, if necessary, for color.

9. Pour the sauce over the quail and garnish with watercress to serve.

Step 1 Rub the inside and outside of each quail with some of the softened butter.

Step 3 Remove the precooked quail from the oven and place under a pre-heated broiler for about 3-4 minutes until golden brown.

Cook's Notes

Time
Preparation takes about 25 minutes and cooking takes about 45-50 minutes.

Serving Ideas
Serve the quail with rice or potatoes and a vegetable accompaniment such as Quick Fried Herbed Vegetables or Minted Mixed Vegetables.

Watchpoint
Quail are very tender birds and can dry out easily. Do not prepare the dish in advance and reheat.

SERVES 6

Cornish Hens with Southern Stuffing

Cornbread makes a delicious stuffing and
a change from the usual breadcrumb variations.

Full quantity Corn Muffin recipe
2 tbsps butter or margarine
2 sticks celery, finely chopped
2 green onions, chopped
2oz chopped country or Smithfield ham
2oz chopped pecans
2 tbsps bourbon
Salt and pepper
1 egg, beaten
6 Cornish game hens
12 strips bacon

Step 3 Add just enough egg to the stuffing mixture to hold it together.

1. Prepare the Corn Muffins according to the recipe, allow to cool completely and crumble finely.

2. Melt the butter or margarine and soften the celery and onions for about 5 minutes over very low heat.

3. Add the ham, pecans, cornbread crumbs and seasoning. Add bourbon and just enough egg to make a stuffing that holds together but is not too wet.

4. Remove the giblets from the hens, if included, and fill each bird with stuffing. Sew up the cavity with fine string or close with small skewers.

5. Criss-cross 2 strips of bacon over the breasts of each bird and tie or skewer the ends of the bacon together.

6. Roast in a pre-heated 400°F oven for 45 minutes – 1 hour, or until tender. Baste the hens with the pan juices as they cook.

7. Remove the bacon, if desired, during the last 15 minutes to brown the breasts, or serve with the bacon after removing the string or skewers.

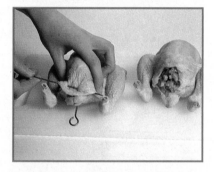

Step 4 Sew up the cavity of the stuffed birds with fine string, or close with small skewers.

Step 5 Criss-cross two strips of bacon over the breast of each bird and tie or skewer the ends together.

Cook's Notes

Time
Preparation takes about 45-50 minutes and cooking takes about 14 minutes for the cornbread and 45 minutes – 1 hour for the hens.

Variation
The stuffing may also be used to stuff a whole chicken or prepared in double or triple quantities for a turkey.

SERVES 4

FRIED CHICKEN

No discussion of Southern cooking is
complete without mentioning fried chicken. Eating
it is even better than talking about it!

3lb frying chicken portions
2 eggs
2 cups flour
1 tsp each salt, paprika and sage
½ tsp black pepper
Pinch cayenne pepper (optional)
Oil for frying
Parsley or watercress

Step 4 Coat the chicken on all sides with flour, shaking off the excess.

Step 2 Dip the chicken pieces in the egg to coat them well.

Step 6 Fry the chicken skin side first for 12 minutes, turn over and fry a further 12 minutes.

1. Rinse chicken and pat dry.

2. Beat the eggs in a large bowl and add the chicken one piece at a time, turning to coat.

3. Mix flour and seasonings in a large paper or plastic bag.

4. Place chicken pieces coated with egg into the bag one at a time, close bag tightly and shake to coat each piece of chicken. Alternatively, dip each coated chicken piece in a

bowl of seasoned flour, shaking off the excess.

5. Heat oil in a large frying pan to the depth of about ½ inch.

6. When the oil is hot, add the chicken skin side down first. Fry about 12 minutes and then turn over. Fry a further 12 minutes or until the juices run clear.

7. Drain the chicken on paper towels and serve immediately. Garnish serving plate with parsley or watercress.

Cook's Notes

Time
Preparation takes about 20 minutes and cooking takes about 24 minutes.

Preparation
The chicken should not be crowded in the frying pan. If your pan is small, fry the chicken in several batches.

Cook's Tip
When coating anything for frying, be sure to coat it just before cooking. If left to stand, coating will usually become very soggy.

SERVES 6

COUNTRY CAPTAIN CHICKEN

A flavorful dish named for
a sea captain with a taste for
the spicy cuisine of India.

3lbs chicken portions
Seasoned flour
6 tbsps oil
1 medium onion, chopped
1 medium green pepper, seeded and chopped
1 clove garlic, crushed
Pinch salt and pepper
2 tsps curry powder
2 14oz cans tomatoes
2 tsps chopped parsley
1 tsp chopped marjoram
4 tbsps currants or raisins
4oz blanched almond halves

1. Remove skin from the chicken and dredge with flour, shaking off the excess.

2. Heat the oil and brown the chicken on all sides until golden. Remove to an ovenproof casserole.

3. Pour off all but 2 tbsps of the oil. Add the onion, pepper and garlic and cook slowly to soften.

4. Add the seasonings and curry powder and cook, stirring frequently, for 2 minutes. Add the tomatoes, parsley, marjoram and bring to the boil. Pour the sauce over the chicken, cover and cook in a pre-heated 350°F oven for 45 minutes. Add the currants or raisins during the last 15 minutes.

5. Meanwhile, toast the almonds in the oven on a baking sheet along with the chicken. Stir them frequently and watch carefully. Sprinkle over the chicken just before serving.

Step 4 Add the curry powder to the vegetables in the frying pan and cook for two minutes over low heat, stirring frequently.

Step 4 Cook the remaining sauce ingredients and pour over the chicken.

Step 5 Toast the almonds on a baking sheet in the oven until light golden brown.

Cook's Notes

 Time
Preparation takes about 30 minutes and cooking takes about 50 minutes.

Preparation
Country Captain Chicken can be prepared completely ahead of time and reheated for about 20 minutes in a moderate oven.

 Serving Ideas
If desired, serve the chicken with an accompaniment of rice.

SERVES 6-8

BRUNSWICK STEW

Peppers, potatoes, corn, tomatoes, onions and lima
beans are staple ingredients in this recipe, which
often includes squirrel in its really authentic version.

3lbs chicken portions
6 tbsps flour
3 tbsps butter or margarine
8oz salt pork, rinded and cut into ¼ inch dice
3 medium onions, finely chopped
3 pints water
3 14oz cans tomatoes
3 tbsps tomato paste
4oz fresh or frozen lima beans
4oz corn
2 large red peppers, seeded and cut into small dice
3 medium potatoes, peeled and cut into ½ inch cubes
Salt and pepper
1-2 tsps cayenne pepper or tabasco, or to taste
2 tsps Worcester sauce
1 cup red wine

1. Shake the pieces of chicken in the flour in a plastic bag
as for Fried Chicken. In a large, deep sauté pan, melt the
butter until foaming. Place in the chicken without crowding
the pieces and brown over moderately high heat for about
10-12 minutes. Remove the chicken and set it aside.

2. In the same pan, fry the salt pork until the fat is rendered
and the dice are crisp.

3. Add the onions and cook over moderate heat for about
10 minutes, or until softened but not browned.

4. Pour the water into a large stock pot or saucepan and
spoon in the onions, pork and any meat juices from the pan.
Add the chicken, tomatoes and tomato paste. Bring to the
boil, reduce the heat and simmer for about 1-1½ hours.

5. Add the lima beans, corn, peppers and potatoes. Add
cayenne pepper or tabasco to taste. Add the Worcester
sauce and red wine.

6. Cook for a further 30 minutes or until the chicken is
tender. Add salt and pepper to taste.

7. The stew should be rather thick, so if there is too much
liquid, remove the chicken and vegetables and boil down
the liquid to reduce it. If there is not enough liquid, add more
water or chicken stock.

Step 3 Add the
onions and cook
slowly until tender
but not browned.

Step 4 Scrape the
contents of the
sauté pan into a
large stock pot or
saucepan of water.

Cook's Notes

 Time
Preparation takes about 1
hour and cooking takes about
2 hours.

Preparation
If desired, prepare the stew
ahead of time, leaving out the
last half hour of cooking. Bring slowly to
the boil and then simmer for about 30
minutes more before serving.

 Freezing
The stew may be frozen for up
to 2 months in rigid
containers. Bring the stew to room
temperature before freezing.

SERVES 2

SAVE-YOUR-MARRIAGE SUPPER

To foster domestic peace anytime, use
this quick and easy recipe to make a
whole meal in one convenient parcel.

2 lamb steaks or 4 rib chops
Oil
1 large potato, scrubbed
4 baby carrots, scraped
1 medium onion, peeled and sliced
1 medium green pepper, seeded and sliced
1 tbsp chopped fresh dill
Salt and pepper

Step 1 Quickly seal and brown the lamb chops in a small amount of oil over high heat.

1. Heat a frying pan and add a small amount of oil. Quickly fry the lamb on both sides to sear and brown.

2. Cut 2 pieces of foil about 12 x 18″. Lightly oil the foil.

3. Cut the potatoes in half and place half on each piece of foil, cut side up.

4. Top with the lamb and place the carrots on either side.

5. Place the onion slices on the lamb and the pepper slices on top of the onions.

6. Sprinkle with dill, salt and pepper, and seal into parcels.

7. Bake at 400°F for about 45 minutes-1 hour, or until the potatoes are tender and the meat is cooked. Open the parcels at the table.

Step 3 Place half a potato on each piece of lightly-oiled foil, cut side up, and place on remaining ingredients.

Step 6 Sprinkle with salt, pepper and dill and seal into parcels.

Cook's Notes

Time
Preparation takes about 30 minutes and cooking takes about 45 minutes-1 hour.

Variation
Other vegetables may be added or substituted. Use sliced parsnips in place of or in addition to the carrots. Substitute a red pepper for the green pepper. Pork chops may also be used, and the cooking time increased by about 15 minutes.

Serving Ideas
This dish is really a complete meal in itself, but add a tomato or green salad for an accompaniment, if desired.

SERVES 8-10

ALABAMA COLA GLAZED HAM

Don't be afraid to try this somewhat
unusual approach to roast ham. Cola
gives it a marvelous taste and color.

10lb joint country or Smithfield ham
4 cups cola soft drink
Whole cloves
1 cup packed dark brown sugar

Step 2 Place the ham rind side down in a roasting pan, pour over the cola and bake.

1. Soak the ham overnight.

2. Preheat oven to 350°F. Place the ham rind side down in a roasting pan. Pour over all but 6 tbsps of the cola and bake, uncovered, 1½ hours or until the internal temperature registers 140°F.

3. Baste the ham every 20 minutes with pan juices using a large spoon or a bulb baster.

4. Remove the ham from the oven and allow it to cool for 10-15 minutes. Remove the rind from the ham with a small, sharp knife and score the fat to a depth of ¼ inch. Stick 1 clove in the center of every other diamond.

5. Mix sugar and the remaining cola together and pour or spread over the ham. Raise the oven temperature to 375°F.

6. Return the ham to the oven and bake for 45 minutes, basting every 15 minutes. Cover loosely with foil if the ham begins to brown too much.

7. Allow to stand 15 minutes before slicing.

Step 4 Remove the rind from the ham with a small, sharp knife. Stick one clove in the center of every other diamond after scoring the fat.

Step 5 Pour or spread the glaze over the ham before continuing to bake.

Cook's Notes

Time
Preparation takes about 30 minutes, with overnight soaking for the ham. Cooking takes about 2 hours 15 minutes.

Serving Ideas
Glazed ham is especially nice served with the Sweet Potato Pudding or Fried Okra. Southern Biscuits or Corn Bread often accompany ham as well.

Preparation
Gammon ham requires overnight soaking to remove saltiness.

SERVES 4 or 8
COUNTRY HAM WITH BOURBON RAISIN SAUCE

The tart and sweet flavor of this sauce has long been the choice to complement savory country ham.

8 slices country or Smithfield ham, cut about ¼ inch thick
Milk
Oil or margarine for frying

Sauce
1½ tbsps cornstarch
1 cup apple cider
½ tsp ginger or allspice
2 tsps lemon juice
2 tbsps bourbon
2oz raisins
Pinch salt

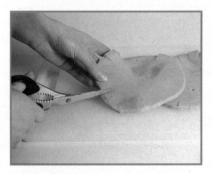

Step 2 Before frying the ham, snip the edges at intervals of ½ inch with kitchen scissors. This will prevent the ham slices from curling.

1. Soak the ham slices in enough milk to barely cover for at least 30 minutes. Rinse and pat dry. Trim off the rind and discard it.

2. Heat a small amount of oil or margarine in a large frying pan and brown the ham slices about 2 minutes per side over medium-high heat.

3. Mix the cornstarch with about 6 tbsps of the apple cider and deglaze the frying pan with the remaining cider. Stir in the ginger or allspice and the lemon juice.

4. Stirring constantly, pour in the cornstarch mixture and bring the liquid to the boil. Cook and stir constantly until thickened. Add the bourbon and raisins and cook a further 5 minutes. Add salt to taste. Reheat the ham quickly, if necessary, and pour over the sauce to serve.

Step 3 Pour the apple cider into the hot pan and scrape to remove any browned meat juices.

Step 4 When the raisins are added to the sauce, cook a further five minutes, or until the raisins are plumped and softened.

Cook's Notes

Time
Preparation takes about 20 minutes, with at least 30 minutes soaking in milk for the ham. Cooking takes about 2 minutes per side for the ham and about 10 minutes for the sauce.

Variation
If desired, cooked ham slices or steaks may be used in place of the country or Smithfield ham. In this case, omit the soaking procedure and simply fry to brown lightly about 1-2 minutes per side. The apple cider you use may be dry or sweet. If using hard or sweet cider, a pinch of sugar will add to the flavor.

Cook's Tip
Soaking country or Smithfield ham in milk will help to remove the saltiness, giving it an improved, milder flavor.

SERVES 4-6

JELLIED AVOCADO SALAD

Salads set with gelatine are
cooling treats in summer or
perfect do-ahead dishes anytime.

Juice of 1 small lemon
1½ tbsps unflavored gelatine
2 ripe avocados
3oz cream cheese or low fat soft cheese
½ cup sour cream or natural yogurt
2 tbsps mayonnaise
3 oranges, peeled and segmented
Flat Italian parsley or coriander to garnish

Step 6 Pour the avocado mixture into oiled custard cups with a piece of wax paper in the bottom.

1. Reserve about 2 tsps of the lemon juice. Pour the rest into a small dish, sprinkle the gelatine on top and allow to stand until spongy.

2. Cut the avocados in half and twist to separate. Reserve half of one avocado with the stone attached and brush the cut surface with lemon juice, wrap in plastic wrap and keep in the refrigerator.

3. Remove the stone from the other half and scrape the pulp from the three halves into a food processor.

4. Add the cheese, sour cream or yogurt and mayonnaise and process until smooth.

5. Melt the gelatine and add it to the avocado mixture with the machine running.

6. Place a small disc of wax paper in custard cups, oil the sides of the cups and the paper and pour in the mixture. Tap the cups lightly on a flat surface to smooth the top and eliminate any air bubbles, cover with plastic wrap and chill until set.

7. Loosen the set mixture carefully from the sides of the cups and invert each onto a serving plate to unmold. Peel and slice the remaining avocado half and use to decorate the plate along with the orange segments. Place parsley or coriander leaves on top of each avocado mold to serve.

Step 7 Make sure the mixture pulls away completely from the sides of the dishes before inverting and shaking to unmold.

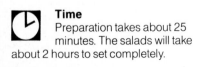

Cook's Notes

Time
Preparation takes about 25 minutes. The salads will take about 2 hours to set completely.

Cook's Tip
Adding lemon juice to the mixture and brushing the avocado slices with lemon juice will help to keep them from turning brown. The salad will discolor slightly even with the addition of lemon juice if kept in the refrigerator more than one day.

Preparation
The avocado salad may be kept in the refrigerator overnight and turned out the next day. Do not keep longer than a day in the refrigerator.

SERVES 6

CABBAGE AND PEANUT SLAW

Boiled dressings are old favorites in
the South. This one gives a lively sweet-
sour taste to basic coleslaw.

1 small head white cabbage, finely shredded
2 carrots, shredded
2 tsps celery seed
1 cup dry-roasted peanuts
1 egg
½ cup white wine vinegar
½ cup water
½ tsp dry mustard
2 tbsps sugar

1. Combine the vegetables, celery seed and peanuts in a large bowl.

2. Beat the egg in a small bowl.

3. Add vinegar, water, mustard and sugar and blend thoroughly.

4. Place the bowl in a pan of very hot water and whisk until thickened. Cool and pour over the vegetables.

Step 3 Add the vinegar, water, mustard and sugar to the egg and blend thorougly.

Step 4 Place in a pan of very hot water and whisk until thickened.

Cook's Notes

Time
Preparation takes about 30 minutes.

Variation
Shredded red cabbage and finely chopped onion may be added to the salad, if desired.

Preparation
The salad may be prepared ahead of time and kept in the refrigerator overnight.

SERVES 6

QUICK FRIED VEGETABLES WITH HERBS

Crisply cooked vegetables with plenty of chives
make a perfect side dish, hot or cold.

4 sticks celery
4 medium zucchini
2 red peppers, seeded
3-4 tbsps oil
Pinch salt and pepper
1 tsp chopped fresh oregano or marjoram
4 tbsps snipped fresh chives

Step 1 Cut the celery sticks into ½ inch slices using a large, sharp knife.

1. Slice the celery on the diagonal into pieces about 1½ inch thick.

2. Cut the zucchini in half lengthwise and then cut into ½ inch thick slices.

3. Remove all the seeds and the white pith from the peppers and cut them into diagonal pieces about 1 inch.

4. Heat the oil in a heavy frying pan over medium high heat. Add the celery and stir-fry until barely tender.

5. Add zucchini and peppers and stir-fry until all the vegetables are tender crisp.

6. Add the salt, pepper and oregano or marjoram and cook for 30 seconds more. Stir in chives and serve immediately.

Step 3 Seed the peppers and cut them into strips. Cut the strips into 1 inch diagonal pieces.

Step 6 Stir-fry all the vegetables, seasonings and herbs until the vegetables are tender crisp.

Cook's Notes

Time
Preparation takes about 25 minutes and cooking takes about 5 minutes.

Preparation
The cooking time for this dish is short, so have everything prepared before actual cooking begins.

Serving Ideas
Serve hot as an accompaniment to Southern Fried Chicken, Cola Glazed Ham or with Cornish Hens with Southern Cornbread Stuffing. Vegetables may also be served cold as a salad with a dash of lemon or lime juice added.

SERVES 4-6

MINTED MIXED VEGETABLES

Carrots, cucumber and zucchini are all
complemented by the taste of fresh mint.
In fact, most vegetables are, so experiment.

Step 5 Combine
all the vegetables
and cook until
liquid is almost
evaporated.

3 medium carrots
1 cucumber
2 zucchini
½ cup water
1 tsp sugar
Pinch salt
1½ tbsps butter, cut into small pieces
1 tbsp coarsely chopped fresh mint leaves

Step 5 Add the
butter, cut in small
pieces and stir
while the liquid
evaporates.

Step 2 Peel the
cucumber, quarter
it and remove the
seed before cutting
into sticks.

1. Peel the carrots and cut them into sticks about ½ inch thick and 2½ inches long.

2. Peel the cucumber and cut it into quarters. Remove the centers and cut into sticks the same size as the carrots.

3. Cut the zucchini into sticks the same size as the other vegetables.

4. Combine the carrots, water, sugar and salt in a medium saucepan. Cover the pan and bring to the boil over high heat. Reduce the heat to medium and cook for about 3 minutes. Uncover the pan and cook a further 3 minutes.

5. Increase the heat and add the cucumber and zucchini and boil until the vegetables are tender crisp. Add the butter and stir over heat until melted and the liquid has completely evaporated, glazing the vegetables. Remove from the heat. add the mint and toss well.

Cook's Notes

Time
Preparation takes about 25-30 minutes and cooking takes about 6-10 minutes.

Variation
Other root vegetables such as parsnips or rutabagas may be used instead of or in addition to the carrots.

Preparation
If the vegetables are cooking faster than the liquid is evaporating, pour off some of the liquid and continue to cook until completely evaporated.

SERVES 4-6

FRIED OKRA

Cornmeal and okra, two Southern specialties, combine in a classic vegetable dish that's delicious with meat, poultry, game or fish.

1 cup yellow cornmeal
1 tsp salt
2 eggs, beaten
1½lbs fresh okra, washed, stemmed and cut crosswise into ½ inch thick slices
2 cups oil for frying

Step 4 Remove the okra from the oil with a draining spoon and place on paper towels.

Step 1 Dredge the egg-coated, sliced okra in the cornmeal and salt mixture.

1. Combine the cornmeal and salt on a plate. Coat okra pieces in the beaten egg. Dredge the okra in the mixture.

2. Place the oil in a large, deep sauté pan and place over moderate heat.

3. When the temperature reaches 375°F add the okra in batches and fry until golden brown.

4. Drain thoroughly on paper towels and serve immediately.

Cook's Notes

Time
Preparation takes about 15-20 minutes and cooking takes about 3 minutes per batch.

Preparation
Do not coat the okra in the cornmeal too soon before cooking. If allowed to stand, cornmeal will become soggy.

Variation

Small okra can be coated and fried whole.

SWEET POTATO PUDDING

All puddings are not necessarily
desserts. This one goes with meat
or poultry for an unusual side dish.

2 medium-size sweet potatoes
2 cups milk
2 eggs
¾ cup sugar
1 tsp cinnamon
¼ cup pecans, roughly chopped
2 tbsps butter
6 tbsps bourbon

Step 3 Pour the mixture into a lightly-buttered shallow baking dish and dot with the remaining butter.

Step 2 When the egg and sugar mixture is light and fluffy, combine it with cinnamon and pecans and add to the potato and milk mixture.

Step 4 Pour the bourbon over the baked pudding just before serving.

1. Peel the potatoes and grate them coarsely. Combine with the milk.

2. Beat the eggs and gradually add the sugar, continuing until light and fluffy. Combine with the cinnamon and the pecans.

3. Stir into the potatoes and milk and pour the mixture into a lightly buttered shallow baking dish. Dot with the remaining butter.

4. Bake about 45 minutes to 1 hour in a pre-heated 350°F oven. Bake until the pudding is set and then pour over the bourbon just before serving.

Cook's Notes

Time
Preparation takes about 25 minutes and cooking takes 45 minutes to 1 hour.

Buying Guide
The sweet potatoes to buy for this recipe are the ones with pale orange or yellow pulp. These are also known as yams in the Southern United States.

Serving Ideas
While this pudding is usually served as a savoury accompaniment to poultry or ham, it can also be served as a sweet pudding with whipped cream or ice cream.

SERVES 6-8

STAINED GLASS DESSERT

Named for the effect of the cubes of colorful gelatine in the
filling, this pretty and light pudding can be made well in
advance of serving.

3oz each of three fruit-flavored gelatine (assorted)
2 cups Graham crackers, crushed
6 tbsps sugar
½ cup butter or margarine
3 tbsps unflavored gelatine
4 tbsps cold water
3 eggs, separated
6 tbsps sugar
4oz cream cheese
Juice and rind of 1 large lemon
½ cup whipping cream

1. Prepare the flavored gelatines according to package directions.

2. Pour into 3 shallow pans and refrigerate until firm.

3. Mix the crushed Graham cracker with the sugar in a food processor and pour melted butter through the funnel with the machine running to blend thoroughly.

4. Press half the mixture into an 8 inch springform pan lined with wax paper. Refrigerate until firm. Reserve half the mixture for topping.

5. Sprinkle the gelatine onto the water in a small saucepan and allow to stand until spongy. Heat gently until the gelatine dissolves and the liquid is clear. Combine the egg yolks, lemon juice and sugar and beat until slightly thickened. Beat in the cream cheese a bit at a time. Pour in the gelatine in a thin, steady stream, beating constantly. Allow to stand, stirring occasionally until beginning to thicken. Place in a bowl of ice water to speed up the setting process.

6. Whip the cream until soft. Whip the egg whites until stiff peaks form and fold both the cream and the egg whites into the lemon-cream cheese mixture when the gelatine has begun to thicken.

7. Cut the flavored gelatines into cubes and fold carefully into the cream cheese mixture.

8. Pour onto the prepared crust. Sprinkle the remaining crust mixture on top, pressing down very carefully.

9. Chill overnight in the refrigerator. Loosen the mixture carefully from the sides of the pan, open the pan and unmold. Slice or spoon out to serve.

Step 7 Fold the cubes of unflavored gelatine carefully into the lemon-cheese mixture using a rubber spatula.

Step 8 Sprinkle reserved crumb topping carefully over the mixture and press down lightly.

Cook's Notes

Time
Preparation takes about 35-40 minutes. Flavored gelatines will take about 1-1½ hours to set, and the finished cake must be refrigerated overnight.

Preparation
Cake may be prepared a day or two in advance and kept in the refrigerator. Do not keep longer than 2 days.

Variation
Use orange juice or lime juice instead of lemon. Alternatively soak the gelatine in water and use vanilla extract to flavor the cream cheese mixture.

SERVES 6

LEMON CHESS PIE

No one is really sure how this zesty
lemon and cornmeal pie came to be so
named, but it's delicious nonetheless.

1½ cups all-purpose flour
Pinch salt and sugar
6 tbsps butter or margarine
2 tbsps plus 1 tsp vegetable shortening
4-5 tbsps cold water

Filling

4 tbsps softened butter
1 cup sugar
3-4 eggs, depending on size
1 tbsp yellow cornmeal
Rind and juice of 1 lemon

Step 9 Lift the pastry around the rolling pin and carefully unroll to lower it into the dish.

1. Sift the flour, salt and sugar into a bowl or process once or twice in a food processor.

2. Add the butter or margarine and shortening and rub into the flour until the mixture resembles fine breadcrumbs, or use the food processor.

3. Add enough water to bring the mixture together in a firm dough. Knead lightly to eliminate cracks, wrap and chill for 30 minutes while preparing the filling.

4. Cream the butter with the sugar until the sugar dissolves.

5. Add the eggs, one at a time, beating well in between each addition.

6. Stir in the cornmeal, rind and juice of the lemon.

7. Roll out the pastry in a circle on a well-floured surface.

8. Roll the pastry carefully onto the rolling pin and transfer to a 9 inch pie or flan dish.

9. Lower the pastry carefully into the dish and press against the sides and base. Trim the edges with a sharp knife if using a pie dish, or roll over the rim of the flan dish with the rolling pin to cut off the excess.

10. Pour in the filling and bake at 350°F for about 45 minutes. Lower the temperature to 325°F if the pie begins to brown too quickly. Cook until the filling sets. Allow to cool completely before serving. Sprinkle lightly with powdered sugar before cutting, if desired.

Step 10 Pour the filling evenly over the base of the unbaked pastry.

Cook's Notes

Time
Preparation takes about 30 minutes and cooking takes about 45 minutes.

Freezing
The pie may be frozen uncooked. Open freeze in the dish and when firm, wrap well and freeze for up to 3 months. Defrost at room temperature and then bake according to the recipe directions.

Serving Ideas
Chess Pie may be served with whipped cream. Decorate the edge of the pie with twisted lemon slices, if desired.

SERVES 6

STRAWBERRY SHORTCAKE

Summer wouldn't be the same without
strawberry shortcake. Add a liqueur to
the fruit for a slightly sophisticated touch.

2 cups all-purpose flour
1 tbsp baking powder
Pinch salt
3 tbsps sugar
6 tbsps cream cheese, softened
3 tbsps butter or margarine
1 egg, beaten
⅓-½ cup milk
Melted butter
1lb fresh or frozen strawberries
Powdered sugar
Juice of half an orange
4 tbsps Eau de Fraises or orange liqueur
1 cup whipped cream

1. Sift the flour, baking powder, salt and sugar into a large bowl.

2. Using 2 knives, forks or a pastry blender, cut in the cheese and butter or margarine. A food processor can also be used.

3. Blend in the egg and enough milk to make a firm dough.

4. Knead lightly on a floured surface and then roll out to a thickness of ½ inch.

5. Cut the dough into an even number of 3 inch circles. Re-roll the trimmings and cut as before. Brush half of the circles with the melted butter and place the other halves on top, pressing down lightly. Bake on an ungreased baking sheet for about 15 minutes in a pre-heated 425°F oven. Allow to cool slightly and then transfer to a wire rack.

6. Hull the strawberries and wash well. Purée half of them

in a food processor with the orange juice and liqueur. Add powdered sugar to taste if desired. Cut the remaining strawberries in half and combine with the purée.

7. Separate the shortcakes in half and place the bottoms on serving plates. Spoon over the strawberries and sauce and pipe or spoon on the cream.

8. Sprinkle the tops of the shortcake with powdered sugar and place on top of the cream. Serve slightly warm or at room temperature.

Step 5 Brush one half of the dough circles with butter and place the other halves on top, pressing down lightly.

Step 7 The shortcakes should separate in half easily with the help of a fork.

Cook's Notes

Time
Preparation takes about 30-35 minutes and cooking takes about 15 minutes.

Variation
Other fruit may be used to fill the shortcakes. Substitute peaches, apricots or other berries. Use orange liqueur or substitute brandy.

MAKES 24

PECAN TASSIES

Like miniature pecan pies, these small
pastries are popular throughout the
Southern states, especially at Christmas.

Pastry

½ cup butter or margarine
6 tbsps cream cheese
1 cup all-purpose flour

Filling

¾ cup chopped pecans
1 egg
¾ cup packed light brown sugar
1 tbsp softened butter
1 tsp vanilla extract
Powdered sugar

1. Beat the butter or margarine and cheese together to soften.

2. Stir in the flour, adding more if necessary to make the dough easy to handle, although it will still be soft. If possible, roll the dough into 1 inch balls. Chill thoroughly on a plate.

3. Mix all the filling ingredients together thorougly, omitting powdered sugar.

4. Place a ball of chilled dough into a small tart pan and, with floured fingers, press up the sides and over the base of the pans. Repeat with all the balls of dough.

5. Spoon in the filling and bake for about 20-25 minutes at 350°F.

6. Allow to cool about 5 minutes and remove carefully from the pans. Cool completely on a wire rack before sprinkling with powdered sugar.

Step 2 Roll the dough into 1 inch balls and chill until firm.

Step 4 Place a ball of dough in a small tart pan and. with floured fingers. press up the sides and over the base.

Step 5 Use a teaspoon to fill the tart pans. taking care not to get filling over the edge of the pastry.

Cook's Notes

Time
Preparation takes about 25 minutes. The dough will take at least 1 hour to chill thoroughly. Cooking takes about 20-25 minutes.

Preparation
If the dough is too soft to handle after mixing, chill for about 30 minutes or until easier to handle.

Variation
If pecans are unavailable, substitute walnuts or hazelnuts.

Serving Ideas
Serve with coffee or tea or as petit fours after a formal dinner. The Tassies can be made in a larger size and served as a dessert with whipped cream.

MAKES 6-8

SOUTHERN BISCUITS

Hot biscuits with butter and sometimes
honey are almost a symbol of Southern
cooking, for breakfast, lunch, dinner or all three!

1¾ cups all-purpose flour
½ tsp salt
2 tsps baking powder
1 tsp sugar
½ tsp baking soda
5 tbsps margarine or 4 tbsps shortening
¾ cup buttermilk

Step 5 Cut the dough into thick rounds with a plain pastry cutter.

Step 2 Rub the fat into the flour until the mixture resembles coarse crumbs. Mix in enough milk to form a soft dough that can be handled.

1. Sift the flour, salt, baking powder, sugar and baking soda into a large bowl.

2. Rub in the fat until the mixture resembles coarse crumbs.

3. Mix in enough buttermilk to form a soft dough. It may not be necessary to use all the milk.

4. Turn the dough out onto a floured surface and knead lightly until smooth.

5. Roll the dough out on a floured surface to a thickness of ½-¾ inch. Cut into rounds with a 2½ inch cookie cutter.

6. Place the circles of dough on a lightly-greased baking sheet about 1 inch apart. Bake in a pre-heated 450°F oven for 10-12 minutes. Serve hot.

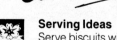
Cook's Notes

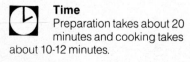
Time
Preparation takes about 20 minutes and cooking takes about 10-12 minutes.

Serving Ideas
Serve biscuits with Southern Fried Chicken, Brunswick Stew, and Cola Glazed Ham. Biscuits are often served hot for breakfast and can be substituted for the shortcake in the Strawberry Shortcake recipe.

Freezing
Biscuits freeze and reheat well. Freeze for up to 3 months and thaw at room temperature. To reheat, wrap in foil and place in a moderate oven for about 5 minutes.

MAKES 12

CORN MUFFINS

A cross between cake and bread, these muffins
are slightly sweet and crumbly. Originally an
Indian recipe, they've become typically Southern.

1 cup all-purpose flour
4 tbsps sugar
2 tsps baking powder
½ tsp salt
1 cup yellow cornmeal
1 egg, slightly beaten
4 tbsps oil
1⅓ cups milk

Step 4 Beat the liquid ingredients in the well with a wooden spoon, gradually incorporating the dry ingredients.

Step 2 Sift the dry ingredients into a large bowl, leaving a well in the center.

Step 5 Spoon the batter into the prepared pans. It may be slightly lumpy.

1. Pre-heat the oven to 450°F. Grease a 12-space muffin tin liberally with oil. Heat the pans for 5 minutes in the oven.

2. Sift the flour, sugar, baking powder and salt into a large bowl. Add the cornmeal and stir to blend, leaving a well in the center.

3. Combine the egg, oil and milk and pour into the well.

4. Beat with a wooden spoon, gradually incorporating the dry ingredients into the liquid. Do not overbeat the mixture. It can be slightly lumpy.

5. Spoon the batter into the pans and bake for about 14 minutes.

6. Cool briefly in the pans and then remove to a wire rack to cool further. Serve warm.

Cook's Notes

Time
Preparation takes about 20 minutes and cooking takes about 14 minutes.

Variation
If you have a cast iron pan, coat liberally with oil and place in the oven to pre-heat. Pour the batter into the pan and then bake. Cut into wedges and serve directly from the pan. The corn muffin recipe may also be used with a corn stick pan. Cut the baking time down to 10-12 minutes.

Freezing
Corn muffins may be baked and frozen well wrapped for up to 2 months. Defrost at room temperature and reheat wrapped in foil for about 5 minutes in a moderate oven. Do not overheat as the muffins can dry out easily. Store well wrapped.

MAKES 5 CUPS

CITRONADE

Nothing surpasses a cold glass of lemonade
in the summer. This is the essential
beverage for picnics and barbecues.

1 lemon
¾ cup sugar
4½ cups water
Maraschino cherries
Lemon slices

Step 3 Pour into glasses or a pitcher with the cherries and lemon slices.

Step 2 Blend with water and sugar in a blender or food processor until smooth.

1. Wash the lemon well and cut into small pieces. removing the seeds. Place in a blender or food processor with the sugar and 1 cup water.

2. Blend until smooth, add remaining water and mix well.

3. Pour into ice-filled glasses or into a pitcher filled with ice and garnish with the cherries and lemon slices.

Cook's Notes

Time
Preparation takes about 20 minutes.

Preparation
Citronade may be prepared well in advance and kept in a refrigerator for several days. If storing for any length of time, do not add the cherries or lemon slices until ready to serve.

Variation
1 small orange may be substituted for the lemon. Cut down the sugar quantity by 4 tbsps. If using limes, substitute 2 limes for the lemon.

MAKES 1 DRINK

MINT JULEPS

The official drink of the Kentucky
Derby, it's mint and bourbon with
a splash of soda – delicious but potent.

2 shots bourbon
3 sprigs of fresh mint
1 tsp sugar
Soda or carbonated mineral water

Step 1 Crush the mint and sugar together in a bowl, glass or jug.

1. Place 1 sprig of mint into a bowl, glass or jug and crush thoroughly with the sugar.

2. Add ⅓-¼ cup of soda or mineral water, mash again and add the bourbon.

3. Pour the mixture through a strainer into a tall glass filled with crushed ice. Stir until the glass frosts, or leave in the refrigerator about 5 minutes. Decorate the glass with the remaining sprigs of mint.

Step 3 Pour through a strainer into a tall glass filled with ice.

Cook's Notes

 Preparation
Mint Juleps are best prepared just before serving. If you wish to partially prepare them in advance, change the order slightly. Crush the required amount of sugar and mint together and then add the bourbon. Crush again and then leave in the refrigerator until ready to add the soda and pour over ice. Mint Juleps can be made in larger quantities.

 Time
Preparation takes about 10 minutes.

 Variation
While not traditional, some recipes for Mint Juleps add a dash of Creme de Menthe.

Index

Alabama Cola Glazed Ham 32
Broiled Flounder 18
Brunswick Stew 28
Cabbage and Peanut Slaw 38
Citronade 60
Corn and Potato Chowder 4
Corn Muffins 58
Cornish Hens with Southern Stuffing 22
Country Captain Chicken 26
Country Ham with Bourbon Raisin Sauce 34
Fried Chicken 24
Fried Okra 44
Jekyll Island Shrimp 12
Jellied Avocado Salad 36
Lemon Chess Pie 50
Mint Juleps 62
Minted Mixed Vegetables 42
Oregano Oysters 14
Pecan Tassies 54
Quick Fried Vegetables with Herbs 40
River Inn Quail 20
Save-your-marriage Supper 30
Sea Island Shrimp 10
She Crab Soup 8
Snapper with Fennel and Orange Salad 16
Southern Biscuits 56
Stained Glass Dessert 48
Strawberry Shortcake 52
Sweet Potato Pudding 46
Virginia Peanut Soup 6

**Compiled by Judith Ferguson
Photographed by Peter Barry
Recipes Prepared for Photography by
Bridgeen Deery and Wendy Devenish**